EL NIÑO
Stormy Weather for People and Wildlife

By CAROLINE ARNOLD

Clarion Books / New York

With thanks to Kevin Trenberth, Head, Climate Analysis Section, Climate
and Global Dynamics Division at the National Center of Atmospheric
Research in Boulder, Colorado; Linda J. Mangum, TAO Project Manager,
Pacific Marine Environmental Laboratory, Seattle, Washington; and Barbara
Massey at California State University, Long Beach, California,
for their help and expert advice.

Clarion Books
a Houghton Mifflin Company imprint
215 Park Avenue South, New York, NY 10003
Copyright © 1998 by Caroline Arnold

Text is 13.5/17-point Galliard.

Printed in Singapore.

LIBRARY OF CONGRESS CATALOGING-IN-PUBLICATION DATA

Arnold, Caroline.
El Niño : stormy weather for people and wildlife / by Caroline Arnold.
p.   cm.   Includes index.
Summary: Explores the nature of the El Niño current and its effects
on people and wildlife.
ISBN 0-395-77602-3
1. El Niño Current—Juvenile literature. 2. Climatic changes—Juvenile literature. [1. El Niño Current. 2. Weather.]
I. Title.
GC296.8.E4A76   1998
551.6—DC21   98-4826   CIP   AC

TWP   10 9 8 7 6 5 4 3 2 1

CONTENTS

Disastrous flooding in southern California in 1992 resulted from unusually heavy rains brought by El Niño.

WACKY WEATHER

For nine straight days in January 1995 rain poured down on the usually sunny state of California, causing floods, mudslides, and power outages. During the same period on the opposite coast flowers began to sprout, bears woke up from their winter naps, and people wore shorts as unusual springlike temperatures warmed the air. Both of these atypical weather events were due to El Niño [pronounced el NEE-nyo], a powerful tropical ocean current that periodically disrupts weather all over the globe. One of the strongest El Niños of this century, in 1982–83, was blamed for hurricanes in Tahiti, floods in the midwestern United States, droughts in South Africa, failed harvests in India, and devastating fires in Australia. That same El Niño also had catastrophic effects on wildlife in many parts of the world as it disrupted ecosystems and played havoc with the food chain. As the most recent El Niño began to develop in the spring of 1997 it showed many similarities to the powerful El Niño of 1982–83. Within the first few months it had caused drought in Southeast Asia, brutal storms and disruption of fisheries in South America, and wildfires in Australia. By midwinter it had brought record-breaking rainfall to California and contributed to devastating tornadoes in Florida. It may prove to be the strongest El Niño in history.

El Niño is the most powerful weather phenomenon on the earth and alters the climate across more than half the planet. The elevated ocean temperatures and changes in weather patterns that we call El Niño occur about every three to seven years. Scientists are only beginning to recognize how these changes develop and spread. Understanding El Niño and its wide-ranging influence is one step in learning how to predict the weather. By anticipating the kinds of alterations that El Niño creates in the weather, we can, in some cases, make preparations to avert their worst consequences.

In any given place the weather changes from day to day and reflects variations in temperature, air pressure, amount of moisture, wind, and other factors. Weather variations occur in part because the sun does not heat all parts of the earth equally, thus creating differences in wind and air pressure. Also, as air moves across the surface of the earth, land forms and bodies of water affect its speed and direction. The seasons of the year and time of

day also influence the weather. The difficulty in predicting the weather is that each of these elements is constantly changing and at the same time influencing and being influenced by the others.

All of the earth's weather is interconnected. An event on one side of the planet can set off a chain of events that changes the weather thousands of miles away. El Niño is part of what meteorologists call the tropical Pacific ocean-atmosphere system and develops from interactions between the ocean and the atmosphere in the tropical Pacific region. El Niño influences weather throughout the Pacific and beyond, but its strongest impact is usually on the coastal regions of western South America.

Fishermen are often the first to notice the effects of El Niño.

WHAT IS EL NIÑO?

El Niño was first noticed in South America and was the name given by Peruvian sailors to a seasonal, warm, southward-moving current along the Peruvian coast. In the southern hemisphere summer begins in December. For centuries fishermen had noticed that at this time of year, the normally cool water along the coast was replaced by a warmer ocean current. Because the warm water usually arrived around Christmas, the fishermen called the phenomenon El Niño, which means "boy child" in Spanish and refers to the Christ child.

In most years the warming of the water is slight, lasts for only a few months, and is limited to a narrow strip along the Peruvian and Ecuadorian coasts. Every few years, however, the increase in water temperature is unusually large. Sea surface temperatures near the equator may rise as much as 5 degrees Centigrade (9 degrees Fahrenheit) above normal, and the pool of warm surface water broadens beyond its usual range to include much of the eastern Pacific. The effects of the unusually elevated water temperature are dramatic. Intense storms associated with the warmer water soak the coastal regions of Peru and Ecuador and provide farmers with bumper crops of fruits and vegetables. For them these seasons of unusually wet weather have long been known as *años de abundancia*, or "years of abundance." For fishermen, on the other hand, a strong El Niño brings disaster. The large schools of anchovies that normally inhabit the cool coastal waters migrate elsewhere. Although some other species remain, they are not populous enough to support the fishing industry. In years of extreme warming the lives of local birds and sea mammals that depend on fish for food are also severely disrupted.

The periodic occurrence of strong El Niños with unusually high ocean temperatures has been known for centuries, but it has only been since the 1960s that scientists have recognized the connection between them and a pattern of abnormal weather events elsewhere in the world. Most people now use the term El Niño only for these years of exceptional warming and use it to refer to the much broader ocean warming of the South Pacific and its associated effects on the weather.

No two El Niños are exactly alike, and the definitions of what makes an El Niño vary depending on what is measured and where the measurements are made. Many scientists use a system created by the Japanese Meteorological Agency (JMA) to define an El Niño year. According to the JMA index an El Niño year is one in which ocean temperatures measured along the equator between 150 degrees east and 90 degrees west (approximately from the eastern tip of Papua New Guinea to the Galápagos Islands off the coast of Ecuador) average more than 0.5 degrees Centigrade (1 degree Fahrenheit) above normal for at least six months.

Watching El Niño

The annual ocean warming noticed by Peruvian fishermen begins in the tropical Pacific, and that is where scientists look for signs of a developing El Niño. By comparing information about present conditions there with information from the past, scientists can better understand new El Niño events.

Before the modern era and use of satellites to gather weather data it was difficult to monitor ocean temperatures. Information could be recorded for periods of time on floating buoys, but then it had to be collected by hand before it could be analyzed. Now it is possible to monitor changes as they happen from thousands of miles away.

Left: *TOPEX/Poseidon satellite, a joint program of NASA and the French space agency, Centre Nationale d'Etudes Spatiales, measures sea surface heights from space.*
Right: *A crew lowers an ATLAS weather buoy into the ocean. It will measure winds and ocean temperatures and transmit via satellite information to researchers and weather forecasters.*

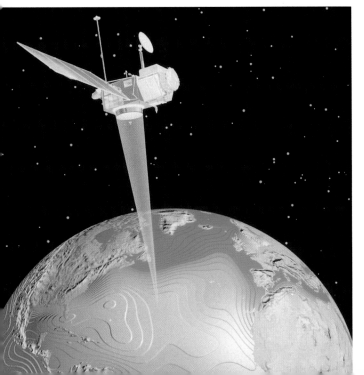 

In 1985 the United Nations World Meteorological Organization established the Tropical Ocean Global Atmosphere (TOGA) program to monitor conditions in the equatorial Pacific. In cooperation with four other nations the National Oceanic and Atmospheric Administration (NOAA) of the United States operates a series of buoys along the equator in the central Pacific. Instruments on the buoys measure surface winds, air temperature, relative humidity, sea surface temperatures, and subsurface temperatures to a depth of 500 meters (1,650 feet). Information is collected daily and sent to weather stations via satellite. It is used both for recording day-to-day changes and for developing computer models that will help forecast the future. Ships that cross this region also collect information and send it to weather centers around the world.

An ATLAS buoy in the central equatorial Pacific.

In an El Niño year tropical moisture moves from the western Pacific toward Hawaii and the coasts of the Americas.

Ocean Warming

The oceans play a large part in regulating the earth's climate. Ocean water, particularly near the equator, is heated by the sun. Unlike air, which cools off quickly when the sun goes down, water releases its heat much more slowly. It acts as a storehouse for the sun's energy. Scientists estimate that the top 3 meters (10 feet) of the ocean contain as much heat as the entire atmosphere. Warm ocean water heats the air above it. The warm air rises, and the moisture in it forms clouds. As this air cools, the moisture condenses and produces rain. The central Pacific Ocean is an important influence on the world's weather because it is the largest expanse of open water on the earth.

Under normal conditions the depth of warm water in the central Pacific is much greater in the west than in the east. The thick layer of warm water in the western Pacific helps to give that region its warm, moist climate. The coastal waters of the eastern Pacific, on the other hand, are much cooler because cold water from the ocean depths is much closer to the surface.

The dividing layer between the upper layers of warm water in the ocean and the deeper, cool water is called the thermocline. In the western Pacific the thermocline may reach depths of up to 150 meters (500 feet), whereas in the eastern Pacific it is only about 50 meters (165 feet) deep. In an El Niño year the thermocline shifts, and the difference between east and west is less. Then the area of heaviest rainfall moves toward the coasts of the Americas.

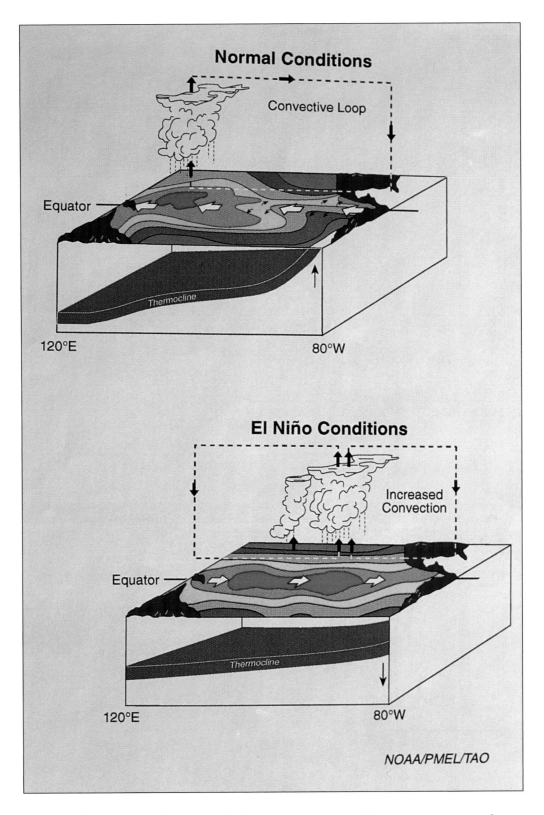

In an El Niño year the areas of the warmest sea surface temperatures, shown in red, enlarge and move to the east. They replace cooler water, shown in green and blue.

13

Changing Winds

Changing wind patterns over the Pacific are another hallmark of El Niño. In the tropics the dominant surface winds, or trade winds, normally blow across the oceans from east to west. As they move across the southern Pacific, they drag warm surface water toward Australia and Indonesia. This wave of warm water actually raises the sea level on the Australian and Indonesian coasts by 30 to 70 centimeters (12 to 28 inches). At the same time, the water level is lowered along the coast of South America. It is the stripping away of warm surface water along the coasts of South America that allows cooler water to reach the surface there.

In an El Niño year the trade winds either subside or change direction and flow east instead of west. Then the warm water that normally accumulates in the western Pacific starts moving toward South America. As this giant wave moves eastward, a trip that takes about two and a half months, it picks up additional heat from the tropical sun. It is this extra heat that provides the fuel for the more violent storms in an El Niño year. At the same time, with heat and moisture removed from the western Pacific, those regions receive less than the normal amount of rainfall and often experience drought.

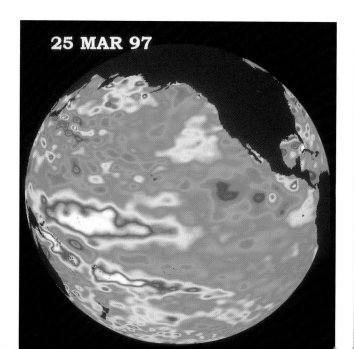
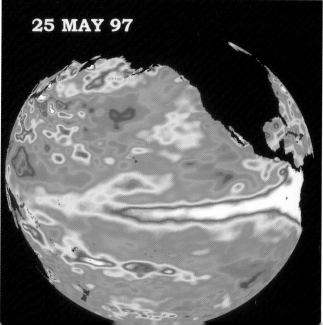

It is thought that two thousand years ago Polynesian sailors took advantage of the westerly winds of El Niño to colonize the islands of the eastern South Pacific.

As the TOPEX/Poseidon satellite orbits the earth it uses radar to get precise measurements of sea surface heights relative to the center of the earth. Scientists use these measurements to produce detailed maps of the ocean surface. On the maps below white represents areas of highest sea level and warmest water temperatures. Purple represents areas that are lower and cooler than normal.

Between March and October 1997 satellite measurements helped track the movement of a large pool of warm water across the Pacific. This shift of warm water from east to west is the hallmark of El Niño. The warm water began to move east from the coast of Australia in March and reached South America one month later. From here the warm water slowly spread northward and by the end of October had reached the shores of Alaska.

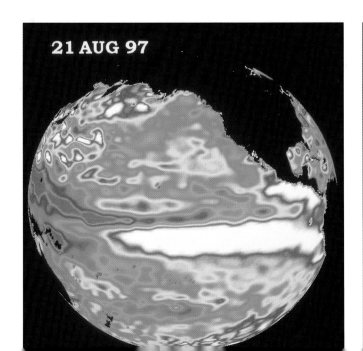

21 AUG 97

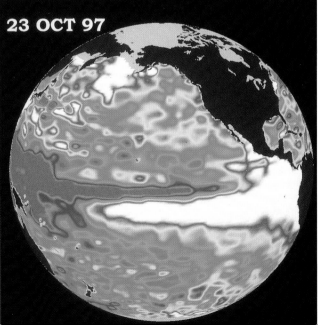

23 OCT 97

The Southern Oscillation

A change in air pressure over the Pacific is another typical feature of El Niño. High air pressure usually means fair skies, whereas low pressure usually indicates clouds and wet weather. The high ocean temperatures in the central Pacific that define an El Niño event usually coincide with an increase in air pressure over the western Pacific. This is the opposite of the usual pattern. Normally air pressure is low over Indonesia and Australia and high over the coast of South America. For reasons that are not yet understood, these conditions reverse every few years. This periodic change in air pressure is called the Southern Oscillation. It is like a giant see-saw of high and low pressure, and like El Niño it has been linked to a wide range of unusual weather events. The combined occurrence of increased ocean temperatures and change in air pressure is frequently referred to as an El Niño/Southern Oscillation, or ENSO, event.

Low air pressure in the western Pacific brings rain to Australian sheep country, whereas long periods of high air pressure lead to drought.

El Niño's "Twin"

Scientists have recently discovered a "twin" of El Niño in the Indian Ocean. Whenever the central Pacific begins warming, signaling the beginning of an El Niño there, they found that water in the Indian Ocean also heats up. At the same time the prevailing winds, which normally blow toward the African coast, shift and blow toward the southeast instead. As warm water moves with the wind toward western Australia, it takes moisture away from India and southern Africa. This simultaneous warming of the Indian Ocean helps explain how El Niño can have such a strong influence on regions beyond the borders of the Pacific. The 1982–83 El Niño was blamed for the worst drought of the century in southern Africa and for the failure of the monsoon rains in southern India.

Nearly all the elephants in Botswana's Chobe National Park died during a drought brought on by the 1982–83 El Niño.

17

An Irregular Schedule

El Niño is a regular weather event that recurs on an irregular schedule. On average an El Niño appears once every three to seven years, but the time between two El Niño events can vary from two to ten years. The length and strength of El Niños also vary. A typical El Niño begins in the northern hemisphere spring or summer and lasts for about a year. Some El Niños, however, last for just a few months, and others stick around for as long as eighteen months.

The El Niño that began in 1991 and eventually subsided in 1995 was considered by many to be the longest El Niño in recorded history. Scientists calculate that such an event is likely to happen only once in every 2,000 years. Not all scientists think that every year in this period qualified as an El Niño year, but most agree that it was an unusual event. Although sea surface temperatures fell back toward the normal range in late 1992 and early 1994, they quickly rose again. Conditions did not return to near normal until July 1995.

The strongest El Niño of the century occurred in 1982–83. It took many people by surprise because even as recently as fifteen years ago, scientists had not studied these conditions well enough to realize the close connection between rising sea surface temperatures in the central Pacific and the later impact of El Niño thousands of miles away. Wildlife in some regions has not yet recovered from the catastrophic changes wrought by that event. The toll in human suffering was also great. The cost of damage caused by flooding, hurricanes, fires, and drought associated with the 1982–83 El Niño is estimated at more than $8 billion. When the impact of the 1997–98 El Niño is totaled, it may well be much greater than that of 1982–83.

Right, top: *El Niño was one of the factors that led to flooding in the midwestern United States in the summer of 1993.*
Right, bottom: *Airey's Inlet, Victoria, Australia. Drought caused by the 1982–83 El Niño contributed to wildfires in Australia that killed 71 people and caused more than $100 million in property damage.*

Scientists detected the beginning of the most recent El Niño in late March 1997. At that time a large pool of warm water that usually stays along the coast of Australia started moving eastward toward South America. As the El Niño developed, sea surface temperatures climbed to levels last seen in 1982–83. As in that strong El Niño, disruptions in weather were soon evident in many parts of the world. Drought in Australia forced cattle ranchers to take their livestock to market earlier than usual and also contributed to devastating wildfires in Sydney. In Malaysia drinking water was in short supply and in Indonesia forest fires were burning out of control. These fires, set to clear land for agriculture, are normally extinguished by the monsoon rains, which, in 1997, didn't occur because of El Niño. Smoke from these fires was blamed for the poor visibility that contributed to an airplane crash in northern Sumatra that killed 234 people in late September.

On the other side of the Pacific, people in South America were experiencing an unusually wet winter. In central Chile, rainfall totals by mid-August were ten times their normal amount. In the Peruvian Andes, snowstorms and freezing temperatures killed 2,500 alpacas, animals that can usually withstand harsh winter weather. Elsewhere, violent storms washed out roads and bridges, downed electric lines, and inundated homes.

In California, the heaviest storms do not usually hit until December or January. The advance prediction of El Niño allowed communities to prepare for its onslaught. Throughout the summer and fall people in California cleaned drains and flood channels, bolstered levees, and repaired leaky roofs while disaster agencies got ready to help people in need. For the first time in history, public awareness of the possible consequences of El Niño gave people the chance to get ready for it. When the worst storms arrived in February there was extensive damage from flooding, mudslides, and high surf. But experts believe that much property damage was averted because of good preparation.

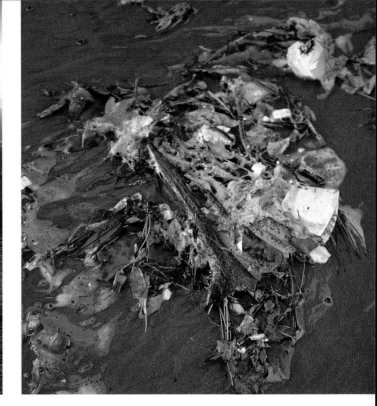

Above, left: *El Niño storms turn flood channels into rivers.*
Above, right: *Trash washed out to sea through storm drains and flood channels often ends up back on the beach.*
Below: *Bulldozers were used to build dikes of sand on Santa Monica beach in California to protect buildings from unusually large waves expected from 1997–98 El Niño storms.*

El Niño and North America

El Niño and ENSO events have their strongest and most direct impact in the lower latitudes, especially in regions bordering the equator in the Pacific. In the temperate latitudes of the world, including those of the United States and Canada, El Niño is just one among a number of factors that affect the weather.

El Niño's influence in North America varies both with its strength and with other weather events. No two weather events are exactly alike, but a typical El Niño brings above-normal rainfall to the southeastern United States and the Gulf Coast, above-normal temperatures to the Pacific Northwest, Alaska, and western Canada, and below-normal temperatures in the southeastern United States. A moderate El Niño, when sea surface temperatures are only slightly above normal, is often associated with extremely dry conditions on the west coast of the United States. Such an El Niño occurred in the winter of 1987–88 and contributed to the California drought of the late 1980s. Strong El Niños, when sea surface temperatures are greatly elevated, such as those of 1940–41, 1982–83, 1991–92, 1993, and 1997–98, bring extremely wet weather to the western United States.

The impact of El Niño on North America is most dramatic in winter, and the strength of the effect depends partly on how it changes the northern hemisphere jet stream, the high-altitude current of fast-moving air that carries weather systems across the continent. Sometimes El Niño pushes the jet stream north over British Columbia. Then as the jet stream dives southward over the middle of the continent, it brings unusually cold air to the Great Lakes region and eastern United States. At the same time, western Canada and the Pacific Northwest have drier than normal weather. In other cases El Niño causes the jet stream to split. Then the northern branch heads north to the Gulf of Alaska, and the southern branch brings storms to California, Texas, and Florida.

Early snow on wheat fields in Alberta, Canada, in 1992 was blamed on El Niño.

La Niña

In the same way that the central Pacific periodically heats up and creates an El Niño, it also sometimes cools down. This mirror opposite of El Niño is called either El Viejo, Spanish for "the old man," or more often La Niña, Spanish for "the girl." (It is also sometimes called an ENSO cold event.) In a La Niña year the sea surface temperatures in the tropical Pacific are unusually cold and the westerly trade winds are particularly strong. According to the JMA index a La Niña year is one in which the average sea surface temperatures are more than 0.5 degrees Centigrade (1 degree Fahrenheit) colder than normal for a period of six months. A La Niña year often follows an El Niño year, but not always. La Niñas occur about once every four years but can be as many as ten years apart.

La Niña generally has an effect on the weather that is opposite that of El Niño. In the United States winter weather in a La Niña year is usually warmer than normal in the southeast and cooler than normal in the northwest. La Niña conditions also seem to favor the formation of hurricanes in the Atlantic. In contrast, El Niño usually coincides with fewer than the normal number of hurricanes, and the likelihood that they will make landfall on the coasts of the United States is reduced.

Left: *Hurricane-whipped waves pound the Florida coast. More hurricanes form in the Atlantic during a La Niña year.*
Right: *In India La Niña brings a monsoon season that is wetter than normal. Farmers need monsoon rains to grow their crops.*

What Triggers El Niño?

Although scientists have made a great deal of progress in learning to recognize El Niño and even to make short-term predictions, they still do not know what causes the higher-than-normal sea warming that triggers an El Niño event.

Some scientists think that undersea volcanoes and lava leaking from deep cracks on the floor of the Pacific Ocean may heat the water enough to start an El Niño. Sonar images of the sea floor near Hawaii and along the East Pacific Rise, a crack extending from the Gulf of California to Easter Island, show lava erupting along the ocean floor. Earthquakes usually coincide with volcanic eruptions, and an increase in the number of earthquakes near Easter Island corresponding to recent occurrences of El Niño suggests that volcanic eruptions in this region may help trigger an El Niño event.

Sunspots may be another factor regulating the onset and length of an El Niño. Recent studies show that the oceans warm and cool according to sunspot cycles. As the sun brightens and dims through its eleven- and twenty-one-year cycles, the small changes in the amount of heat energy reaching the earth may be enough to change ocean temperatures.

Left: *Sunspots represent storm activity on the surface of the sun and appear as deep, dark holes.*
Right: *The ocean floor near Easter Island has the greatest concentration of active volcanoes on the earth.*

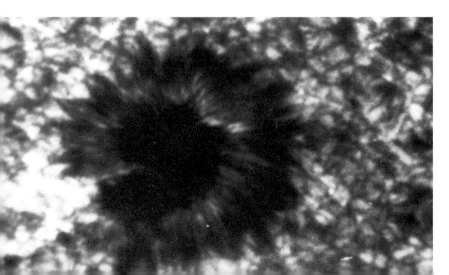

EL NIÑO AND WILDLIFE

Sea life is abundant along the coasts of the eastern Pacific because of the cool water there. As easterly winds blow the warm surface water away from shore, colder water rises to replace it, a phenomenon known as upwelling. The cold water is rich in chemical nutrients, and as it reaches sunlight, tiny plants called phytoplankton use the nutrients to grow and multiply. The phytoplankton becomes food for tiny sea animals called zooplankton, which in turn are eaten by small fish and other sea animals. At the top of the food chain are larger fish, birds, sea mammals, and people.

In an El Niño year, when upwelling is prevented by the thick layer of warm water along the coast, nutrients do not reach the surface, and the food chain is broken. Then the inhabitants of this ecosystem must go elsewhere for food, find other resources, or

starve. The changes in food supplies resulting from El Niño weather events can send ripples along the food chain that last for several years. Although the most obvious effects of El Niño on wildlife are seen along the coasts of South America, plant and animal life throughout the Pacific region can be affected by the warm water of an El Niño sea.

Sea life is also affected by the violent storms that often accompany El Niño. Large ocean waves can erode the shoreline or damage the places where the animals live. Also, when flooded rivers wash into the sea, they bring silt and other contaminants into the water.

The El Niño of 1982–83 was notable for its extreme effects on wildlife. Magellanic penguins, which live in the coastal waters of Peru and Chile, went hungry when the fish they depended on for food disappeared.

Left: *A male California least tern offers a fish to his mate.*
Right: *The female typically lays two eggs in a sandy nest.*

Sea Birds

Sea birds, which depend on fish and other ocean life for food, are among the most directly affected by changes in the ecosystem caused by El Niño. When there are fewer fish to catch in the warm water of an El Niño sea, the birds have a harder time getting enough to eat and find it more difficult to raise their young. For many species of sea birds the severe El Niño of 1982–83 had disastrous consequences. On Christmas Island in the central Pacific 7 million sea birds abandoned their nests. In the United States the California least tern was one of many kinds of sea birds that suffered in 1982–83. This endangered species nests each spring and summer on beaches along the California coast.

At the beginning of the breeding season California least terns gather in colonies, each pair making its nest in a shallow scrape in the sand. In 1982 scientists studying a nesting colony of California least terns at Venice Beach in Los Angeles began to notice changes in the birds' behavior. The season began as usual

California least tern parents take turns bringing food to their hungry chicks.

with the males courting the females by bringing them "gifts" of fish. Compared to previous years, however, these fish were unusually small, indicating that food was hard to find. When the females laid their eggs, they did so late, laid fewer, and abandoned more of them. The chicks that hatched developed poorly, and many more died. Then, to make matters worse, an American kestrel, a predator of small birds, caught and killed a large number of least tern chicks.

Although the food supplies for the California least tern returned to normal in 1983, the effects of the bad breeding season in 1982 were felt for several years. California least terns do not begin breeding until they are two or three years old. So in 1984 and 1985, with many fewer birds in this age group, the number of chicks was still lower than normal. It was not until the 1988 breeding season that the colony began to recover from the effects of the 1982 El Niño.

Coral Reefs

With their brilliant colors and branching shapes, coral reefs resemble beautiful undersea gardens. Although plantlike in their appearance, the reefs are actually the hard outer skeletons of tiny tube-shaped animals called coral polyps. The coral polyps live inside hard structures that they make from calcium carbonate, a mineral found in seawater. Most coral species grow only in the shallow warm water of tropical oceans.

Corals are extremely sensitive to changes in their environment and can be killed if the surrounding water becomes either too cold or too hot, even if the difference is just a few degrees. When the corals die, the colors disappear from the outer skeletons and leave them white, as if they had been bleached. The most widespread coral bleaching ever known occurred in 1982–83, when the water in the eastern Pacific rose 2 to 3 degrees Centigrade (4 to 5 degrees Fahrenheit) above normal. Many corals died, and some species became extinct.

Scientists who study coral reefs believe that El Niño may be one of the most important influences on reef building in the eastern Pacific. Damage caused by the 1982–83 El Niño to coral reefs in the eastern Pacific was particularly severe off the coasts of Costa Rica, Panama, Colombia, Ecuador, and the Galápagos Islands. Some of the reefs were estimated to be at least three hundred years old. Before succumbing to the conditions created by the 1982 event, they had apparently survived at least three centuries of less severe El Niños. This suggests that El Niños with extremely high temperatures may occur only every 200 to 500 years. If that is true, then the recent appearance of record-high sea temperatures in 1997 is highly unusual. By mid-1997 more coral reefs in Panama, Costa Rica, and Mexico were dying, adding to damage begun in 1982–83.

Above: *Coral reefs near the Galápagos Islands were badly damaged by the 1982–83 El Niño.*

Below: *The bleached skeleton of a staghorn coral.*

Marine Iguanas

The 1982–83 El Niño also had disastrous consequences for the Galápagos marine iguana. These reptiles, which can grow to be more than a meter long (39 inches), are unique to the Galápagos Islands. The main food of these large, stocky lizards is the fleshy red algae that grow on rocks at the edge of the sea. In 1982–83 all the red algae died because they could not tolerate the higher water temperatures. They were replaced with brown algae that thrive at warmer temperatures. The marine iguanas could not digest the brown algae and starved.

More than half of the marine iguanas of the Galápagos Islands died of starvation during the 1982–83 El Niño.

Kelp forests provide shelter for fish and other sea life.

Kelp Forests

Giant kelp forests along the California coast are another type of ocean community that does not do well in an El Niño year. Although kelp's long fronds make it look like a leafy plant, it is actually a type of alga. Kelp attaches itself to rocks at the bottom of the ocean and then grows up to the surface, sometimes reaching lengths of more than 60 meters (200 feet). Kelp feeds on tiny organisms suspended in the water. When the water becomes excessively warm, as it did in 1982–83, these organisms die and the kelp starves. Ocean warming in the summer of 1997 again reduced the nutrients in water along the California coast. The Monterey Bay Aquarium, which normally pumps untreated seawater into its kelp forest display, had to add supplements to the water to keep the kelp healthy.

Kelp can also be damaged by the violent storms that often accompany El Niño or La Niña. The effects of El Niño or La Niña can be quite severe on kelp forests, but most colonies quickly regrow when conditions return to normal.

A Galápagos sea lion mother nurses her pup. When food is plentiful, the animals are sleek and healthy.

Sea Mammals

Fish-eating sea mammals also frequently suffer from the effects of El Niño. When fish disappear from their usual feeding areas, many animals go hungry. The 1982–83 El Niño was especially bad for sea lions and fur seals living in the Galápagos Islands and along the South American coasts. The young animals suffered the most. Many newborns died because their mothers spent so much time at sea, trying to find fish for themselves, that their pups did not get enough milk. Pups that did survive were weak and later died because they did not have the skills to find their own food. Many territorial males also died. During the breeding season male seals and sea lions do not eat for several weeks while they defend their breeding territories. Food was so scarce in 1982–83 that when the males went back to sea after breeding, many did not regain enough strength to last through the year.

The El Niño of 1997–98 was unusually bad for sea mammals living along the California coast. One breeding colony, on San Miguel Island, near Santa Barbara, had between 85,000 and 180,000 sea lions and 11,000 fur seals in it. Mothers in both species gave birth to pups in early summer. As water temperatures rose during the summer of 1997, mothers had an especially hard time finding food. Anchovies, which are the staple food of sea lions and fur seals, had migrated to cooler waters, and other fish species, such as halibut and rockfish, had moved to depths beyond the diving range of the animals. Both mothers and pups went hungry. By December 6,000 pups had died and few of those that remained were expected to survive the season. Female sea lions and fur seals normally breed for about twenty years of their lives and produce one pup a year. If a large proportion of the adult females die as well, it may be many years before the population recovers.

When sea mammals are sick or injured, they often come to shore and beach, or strand, themselves. During an El Niño year sea mammal rescue stations on the California coast are inundated by large numbers of stranded sea lions, elephant seals, fur seals, and harbor seals. At the rescue center the animals receive food, water, and medical care. In most cases the animals recover and are later released.

Left: *Sea lion rescuers in California use large nets to catch the animals and sturdy cages to transport them safely back to the shelter.*
Right: *Regular feedings usually bring stranded sea lions back to health quickly.*

Foxes

Red foxes that live on Round Island, Alaska, in the Bering Sea, provide another example of the far-reaching influence of El Niño. Foxes normally thrive on Round Island because it is protected from most predators and has abundant food and plenty of sites to make dens. In summer the foxes feast on sea birds that nest on the island's rocky cliffs. Usually more than 100,000 sea birds nest on Round Island during the summer months. The most numerous species, common murres and black-legged kittiwakes, nest in large colonies and are easily preyed upon by the foxes. The foxes feed the meat to their growing pups. They also store some of the birds' eggs in holes in the tundra and save them for winter.

Every few years, however, the sea and air of the Bering Sea grow warmer, an event coinciding with El Niño. At these times the murres and kittiwakes that normally nest on the cliffs of Round Island fail to do so. And although there are some other species that nest on the island, they are smaller and more difficult for the foxes to catch. With less food available the foxes cannot raise as many pups. Scientists studying the foxes of Round Island discovered that in comparison to abundant years, when the foxes may have as many as seven litters with more than four pups in each, there may be only one litter with only three or four pups in an El Niño year. So even thousands of miles from the tropics, El Niño can be a factor in whether or not animals can raise their young successfully.

Red fox.

Flooding in the Brazilian rain forest.

THE DISEASE CONNECTION

With both El Niño and La Niña, climate extremes become more intense, so droughts are more severe and floods are more frequent. Drought leads to famine and diseases associated with malnutrition. Flooding promotes the increase of waterborne diseases such as cholera and typhoid. Prolonged wet periods are also favorable for the breeding of insects that carry diseases such as malaria and encephalitis. After the 1982–83 El Niño caused heavy rain and flooding in Ecuador, Peru, and Bolivia, the mosquitoes multiplied and there were major outbreaks of malaria. La Niña can also cause unusual wet periods. The 1973–74 La Niña caused an especially wet summer in southern Africa and contributed to an epidemic of West Nile fever there. That same year wet conditions in Brazil resulted in an outbreak of encephalitis in which sixty-one people died.

In the spring of 1993 a mysterious and deadly disease appeared in rural areas of the Four Corners region of the southwestern United States (where Arizona, New Mexico, Utah, and Colorado meet). Scientific sleuthing quickly identified the cause of the flu-like disease, a type of virus called the hantavirus; but the real culprit turned out to be El Niño. El Niño conditions in the previous spring had brought unusually heavy rains to the desert, promoting heavy growth of desert plants. Small rodents called deer mice feasted on the abundant food and multiplied. Ordinarily, predators such as owls and snakes keep the number of deer mice under control. But a six-year drought that preceded the heavy rains had reduced their numbers and allowed the deer mouse population to grow unchecked.

Deer mice are carriers of the hantavirus. Although the virus lives in their bodies, it does not make them sick. Most of the people who became infected with the hantavirus either lived or worked in remote locations where deer mice were common. The people became exposed to the virus when they touched deer mouse droppings or breathed contaminated dust. The outbreak quickly subsided as the desert climate returned to normal, food became scarce, and the deer mouse population returned to normal.

Abundant plant growth in the deserts of the southwestern United States in the spring of 1992 contributed to a population explosion of deer mice.

Coral reefs provide clues to seasonal temperature variations in tropical oceans.

PAST AND FUTURE

El Niño is a weather event that has been around for thousands of years or longer. Accounts by Spanish explorers in South America provide information about El Niños as far back as the late sixteenth century. Another way that scientists learn about El Niños of the past is by looking for their effects on the environment.

In the southwestern United States the heavy rains that promote rapid growth usually occur in El Niño years. Growth rings of trees can show which years were particularly rainy. As a tree grows, it produces rings—a light ring in spring and a dark ring in summer. Because the rings are wide in wet seasons and narrow in dry seasons, they reveal the pattern of weather during a tree's life.

Tropical corals also reveal the patterns of past El Niños. Corals add a new growth band each year. The chemical makeup of each band reveals the temperature and saltiness of the water during the year in which the band formed. A large coral reef may represent centuries of growth.

Glaciers, like this one in the Canadian Rockies, accumulate new layers of ice each year, providing a record of each year's temperatures and snowfall.

Glacial ice cores, ocean sediments, and erosion of rocks in ancient river bottoms are some of the other sources scientists use to get information about weather events in the past. During the past 10,000 years the climate has often shifted from hot to cold and wet to dry. Some experts in ancient climate patterns think that shifts in prehistoric El Niño currents may have been linked to those dramatic changes in temperatures and rainfall.

Some people wonder whether the recent El Niños, which have been either longer or stronger than usual, are the result of global warming. Average global temperatures have increased by about 0.5 degrees Centigrade (1 degree Fahrenheit) over the past hundred years, and the ten warmest years of the century have occurred in the last fifteen years. Too much is still unknown to determine whether there is a connection between the occurrence of El Niño and possible global warming. The climate extremes that accompany El Niño may, however, provide a preview of what we might experience if the planet warms up.

Weather and climate patterns of the past help scientists predict the future. Scientists at the National Weather Service Climate Analysis Center and at the National Oceanic and Atmospheric Administration (NOAA) use information from past weather events to create computer models of the earth's weather. Some of these models are able to predict general climate conditions as many as twelve to eighteen months in advance and in some cases to forecast El Niños. These predictions are helping people to better manage agriculture, water supplies, fisheries, and other resources that are affected by the weather.

One country that has benefited from El Niño forecasts is Peru. Each year since 1983 the Peruvian government has used information about winds and water temperatures in the Pacific to make predictions for the upcoming rainy season. Farmers are told to expect one of four possibilities: near-normal conditions, a weak El Niño with a slightly wetter than normal growing season, a full-blown El Niño with flooding, or cooler-than-normal ocean temperatures with a higher-than-normal chance of drought. They then use this information to decide what combination of their two major crops, rice and cotton, they should plant. Rice does well in wet conditions, whereas cotton, which has a deeper root system, can tolerate drier weather. By adjusting the amounts and varieties of each crop according to predicted conditions, the farmers can improve their harvests. Other countries that have used El Niño predictions to manage agriculture are Australia, Brazil, Ethiopia, and India.

Above: *Rice plants need a moist environment for growth.*
Below: *Cotton plants thrive in a warm, relatively dry climate.*

Until recently El Niño was thought to be a local occurrence on the South American coast. Now scientists realize that it is the force behind a wide range of weather events all across the globe. El Niño is the most important influence on world weather beyond the annual cycle of the seasons. As scientists find out about El Niño, La Niña, and the Southern Oscillation, they are learning how ocean warming that begins in the tropical Pacific is one of the most important keys to understanding the earth's weather.

El Niño storm clouds clear over Santa Monica beach, California.

44

EL NIÑO AND LA NIÑA SINCE 1950*

El Niño Events			La Niña Events		
Begin	End	No. of Months	Begin	End	No. of Months
Aug 1951	Feb 1952	7	Mar 1950	Feb 1951	12
Mar 1953	Nov 1953	9	Jun 1954	Mar 1956	22 }
Apr 1957	Jun 1958	15	May 1956	Nov 1956	7
Jun 1963	Feb 1964	9	May 1964	Jan 1965	9
May 1965	Jun 1966	14	Jul 1970	Jan 1972	19
Sep 1968	Mar 1970	19	Jun 1973	Jun 1974	13 }
Apr 1972	Mar 1973	12	Sep 1974	Apr 1976	20
Aug 1976	Mar 1977	8 }	Sep 1984	Jun 1985	10
Jul 1977	Jan 1978	7	May 1988	Jun 1989	14
Oct 1979	Apr 1980	7	Sep 1995	Mar 1996	7
Apr 1982	Jul 1983	16			
Aug 1986	Feb 1988	19			
Mar 1991	Jul 1992	17 }			
Feb 1993	Sep 1993	8			
Jun 1994	Mar 1995	10			
Apr 1997**					

*El Niño and La Niña events are defined as periods when the sea surface temperature measured in the region between 5 degrees north and 5 degrees south and between 120 degrees and 170 degrees west varied 0.4 degrees Centigrade from average for six months or more. Events are joined by brackets when the periods in between remained higher or lower than normal but not enough to qualify as El Niño or La Niña. (From "The Definition of El Niño," by Kevin Trenberth, *Bulletin of the American Meteorological Society,* December 1997, pages 2771–77.)

**As this book went to press in early 1998, the El Niño that began in April 1997 was still at full strength. It was expected to subside by the end of 1998.

FOR FURTHER REFERENCE

You can get up-to-date information about El Niño on the internet at http://www.pmel.noaa.gov/toga-tao/el-nino/home.html

You can also find out about El Niño and more about the weather in the following publications:

"What Is Happening to El Niño?" by Kevin Trenberth, *Yearbook of Science and the Future* (Encyclopedia Britannica, 1997), pp. 89–98

How the Weather Works by Michael Allaby (Reader's Digest, 1995)

Weather: Mind-Boggling Experiments You Can Turn into Science Fair Projects by Janice Vancleave (John Wiley and Sons, 1995)

The Amateur Meteorologist: Explorations and Investigations by Michael Mogil and Barbara G. Levine (Franklin Watts, 1993)

Weather and Climate, Time-Life Understanding Science and Nature series (Time-Life, 1992)

Looking at Weather by David Suzuki with Barbara Hehner (John Wiley and Sons, 1991)

Skywatch: The Western Weather Guide by Richard A. Keen (Fulcrum, Inc., 1987)

"El Niño's Ill Wind" by T. Y. Canby, *National Geographic* (February 1984), pp. 144–183

GLOSSARY

algae–small plants that grow in the water.

años de abundancia–Spanish words meaning "years of abundance." In these years heavy rainfall along the coasts of South America helps to produce large harvests.

ATLAS–Autonomous Temperature Line Acquisition System. Oceanographic moored buoys developed by NOAA to measure and transmit in real time information about winds and ocean temperatures to researchers and weather forecasters.

climate–the prevailing, or average, weather conditions of a region or zone.

coral polyp–the living part of coral. Colonies of coral polyps and their hard outer skeletons form a coral reef.

East Pacific Rise–a crack in the earth's surface along the sea floor, extending from the Gulf of California to Easter Island.

ecosystem–a particular environment and the plants and animals that live in it.

El Niño–Spanish words meaning "the boy." Unusually warm water along the coast of South America; also, a recurrent set of climate conditions linked to unusually warm water in the central Pacific.

El Viejo–Spanish words meaning "the old man." The term for the set of climate conditions linked with unusually cold water in the central Pacific. Also called La Niña.

ENSO–El Niño/Southern Oscillation. A term that refers to the combined occurrence of high ocean temperatures in the central Pacific and a shift in high air pressure from east to west.

hurricane–a severe circular storm that forms over the ocean; in the western Pacific and Indian ocean these storms are called typhoons.

jet stream–the high-altitude currents of fast-moving air that carry weather systems from west to east across the upper latitudes of the northern and southern hemispheres.

JMA–Japanese Meteorological Agency. This agency monitors weather in Japan and the Pacific.

kelp–large, coarse, brown seaweed.

La Niña–Spanish words meaning "the girl." A term for the set of climate conditions linked with unusually cold water in the central Pacific. Also called El Viejo.

monsoon–a seasonal rainy period in south Asia.

NOAA–National Oceanic and Atmospheric Administration. This agency, which is part of the United States Department of Commerce, monitors weather in the United States.

phytoplankton–microscopic plants found floating in water. In the presence of sunlight they use chemical nutrients in the water to make food.

sonar–an apparatus that transmits high-frequency sound waves in water and registers the vibrations reflected back from an object; can be used to detect objects in the ocean or formations on the sea floor.

Southern Oscillation–the periodic eastward shift of air pressure over the Pacific Ocean.

sunspots–dark areas that appear on the surface of the sun, indicating regions of solar storms.

temperate latitudes–the regions of the earth located between the tropics and the polar circles.

thermocline–the dividing layer in the ocean between the upper layers of warm water and the deeper cool water.

TOGA–Tropical Ocean Global Atmosphere program. This program monitors weather conditions in the equatorial Pacific.

trade winds–the dominant surface winds across the ocean. They normally blow from east to west.

tropics–the region of the earth located between the Tropic of Cancer and the Tropic of Capricorn.

upwelling–the rising of deeper, cool water to the surface of the ocean.

weather–the state of the air or atmosphere at a given time and place with respect to temperature, pressure, humidity, cloudiness, and any other meteorological condition.

zooplankton–microscopic animal life found floating or drifting in the water.

INDEX

Page numbers in *italics* refer to illustrations or captions

Photo and Illustration Credits